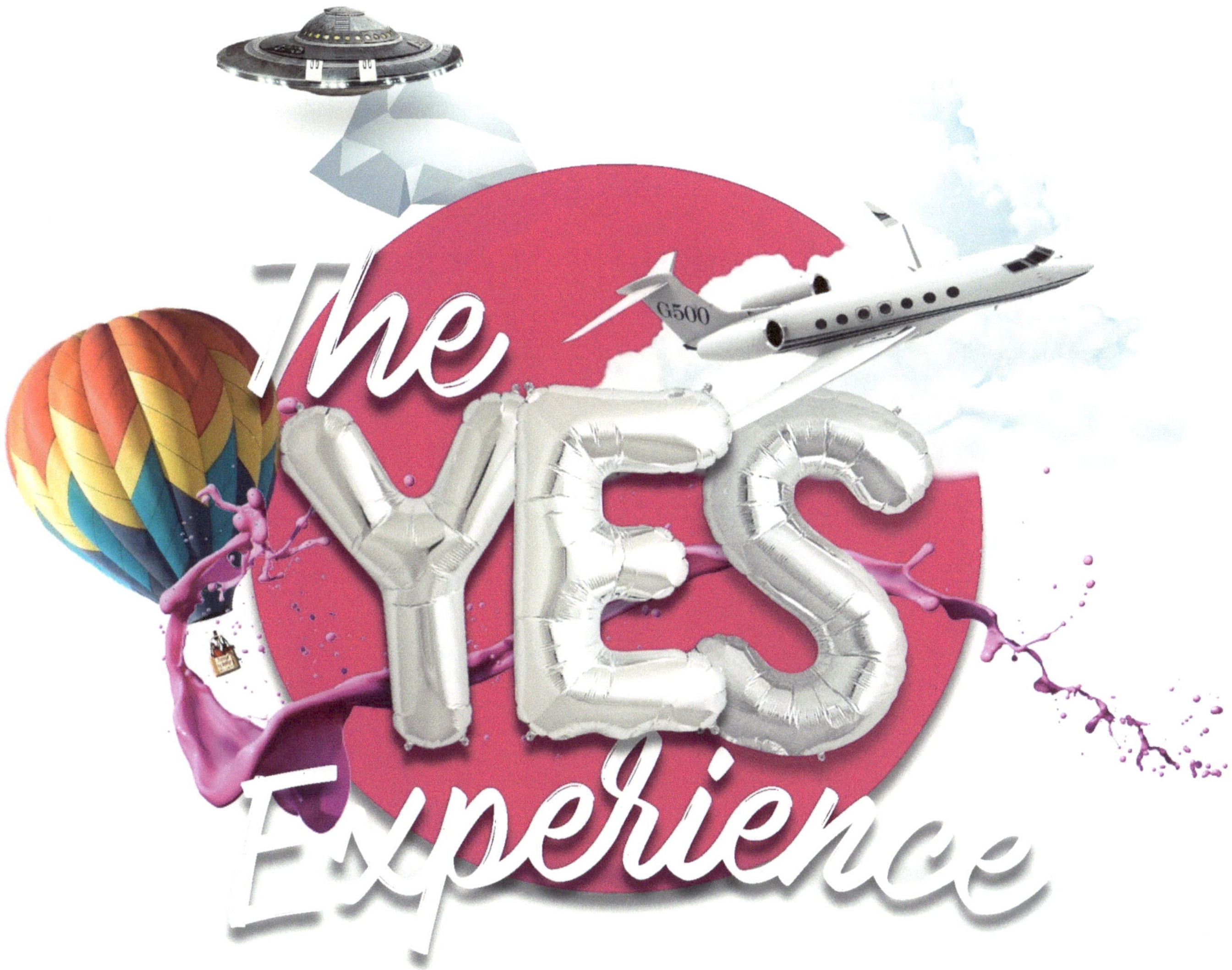

The YES Experience

AUDRIA RICHMOND
BRANDING AND MARKETING GENIUS

COPYRIGHT

The Yes Experience

By

Audria Richmond

Founder and CEO of Building BIG Brands Agency & UnCloned LIfe

COPYRIGHT ©2017-2018 BUILDING BIG BRANDS PUBLISHING
ALL RIGHTS RESERVED

All rights reserved. No part of this publication may be reproduced, distributed, or transmitted in any form or by any means, including photocopying, recording, or other electronic or mechanical methods, without the prior written permission of the publisher, except in the case of brief quotations embodied in critical reviews and certain other noncommercial uses permitted by copyright law. For permission requests, email the publisher, addressed "Attention: Permissions Coordinator," at the following email, info@buildingbigbrands.com

Building BIG Brands Publishing
info@buildingbigbrands.com
www.audriarichmond.com

Ordering Information:

Special discounts are available on quantity purchases by corporations, associations, and others. For details, contact the publisher at the email address above.

Orders by U.S. trade bookstores and wholesalers. Please contact Building BIG Brands Publishing:

**Tel: (901) 238-6859; or
visit www.audriarichmond.com**

**(Paperback)
ISBN 13:** 978-0-9980722-3-4
ISBN: 10 0-9980722-3-0

**Developmental Editing by: Stefanie Manns
Proofreader: Apryl Beverly
Cover Design by: Rochelle Sodipo Washington
Interior Design by: Rochelle Sodipo Washington**

WHY DID I CREATE The YES Experience?

"THE FIRST STEP TO ANYTHING GREAT IS THE FIRST STEP"
—AUDRIA RICHMOND

If I say I'm going to make something happen, you can consider it done. So it should come as no surprise the people who I roll with are doers too. But the more people I have an opportunity to connect and converse with outside of my inner circle, the more I realize too many people are still sitting on the sidelines of their lives, wishing and waiting for things to happen, as opposed to running down the field, scoring.

The truth is, we are all striving for success in our lives. We all want to do something, create something, be something, and get something. There is a light in our eyes and vision on our hearts.

We want something so bad we can taste it, see it, and feel it. We have the vision for the dream business that serves millions of people and makes millions of dollars, the big, five-bedroom house with the designer dog and the manicured yard, or the "sweep-me-off-my-feet marriage" that makes soap-opera romances look like puppy love.

You see, what binds us is the vision, the dreams, and the desires. But, honestly, the action is what separates us. Sadly, people spend more time hoping for success rather than spending the time doing what it takes to achieve it.

I am fortunate to be a self-starter. If I want something, I write it down, plan it out, and leap. I love the excitement of creating something in my head and bringing it to life. I am willing to lose sleep, friends, "grown-folks time" with my husband (fortunately, he's usually grinding right beside me), television shows—you name it, to accomplish something that I set out to do.

"VISION WITHOUT ACTION IS JUST A DREAM, ACTION WITHOUT VISION JUST PASSES THE TIME, AND VISION WITH ACTION CAN CHANGE THE WORLD". -NELSON MANDELA

I am a doer and a finisher. However, in working with and talking to so many different people in business and life, I've found that many people get stuck in the midst of the action ... the part that involves making BIG things happen.

Now, when I was introduced to the vision board concept a few years ago, I instantly fell in love with the idea. For me, it was the first time I sat down and thought about my big goals, the ones that may take months, even years to achieve. I believe the traditional vision board is phenomenal for giving people an opportunity to see their desires mapped out in an eclectic collection of pictures and motivational words.

However, it's still a flat representation of our wants. You see, our desires are multi-dimensional. They have feelings attached to them. They shift and move. They evolve, just like we do. While the vision board is a great start, we need something bigger to capture every aspect of the complex evolution of real life.

So I created the Yes! Board with the intention of revolutionizing how we map out our visions. It did what I set out to do, which was to give people a tool that can grow as their life changes and goals expand. My followers loved it, but it wasn't long before I knew we still needed to go deeper. We needed to answer the question that was at the core of it all:

ONCE WE SEE IT, THEN WHAT?

Seeing the vision was great, but most of us need more than a collection of pretty pictures to demonstrate our desires. We need a plan. Because lack of planning is the real reason people don't take the necessary steps to achieve the "yes."

Failure isn't always a result of not doing the work. More often it's a result of just not knowing which work to do.

The Yes! Experience is where the vision meets the work.

In this course, we'll explore the self-reflection, self-motivation, and planning needed to get to your "yes." Whether you want to lose your first six pounds or build a six-figure business doing something you love, The Yes! Experience will finally show you a repeatable process for getting to your "yes" with ease. Together, we will see it, believe it, and, most importantly, we'll do it.

Step inside The Yes! Experience.

HOW TO GET THE *Course*

CLAIM YOUR COURSE

When I created this course, the one thing I was sure about was my dedication to deliver something more than anything that you'd ever experienced when it came to creating a vision for yourself and your life.

So as a member of The Yes! Experience crew, you'll have access to exclusive features and benefits that will support every twist and turn of your journey, including:

- A digital membership portal with worksheets, video trainings, and other tools and resources

- A close-knit Facebook community of other vision-fueled people to do the work alongside you

- A live, monthly call with me and other members to ask questions, and share any obstacles and progress towards your goals

- And more to come!

HOW TO GET THE *Course*

LET'S START THE PARTY

It's now time to get this party started. Please use the instructions below to activate your YES! Experience.

Step One:
Please visit www.theyesparty.com

Step Two:
Create your username and password.

Step Three:
Login into your account and access the content

Step Four:
Please click **"Join Group"** inside of the membership portal. Can't wait to party with you!

KNOWING *yourself*

CUT + PASTE
A PHOTO OF YOURSELF

WRITE DOWN YOUR
BACKGROUND & HISTORY

WHAT DO YOU LOVE ABOUT YOURSELF?

WRITE DOWN YOUR
PERSONAL BIO

WHAT WOULD YOU LIKE TO IMPROVE ABOUT YOURSELF?

WRITE DOWN A STORY OF YOUR FUTURE SELF

FOCUS

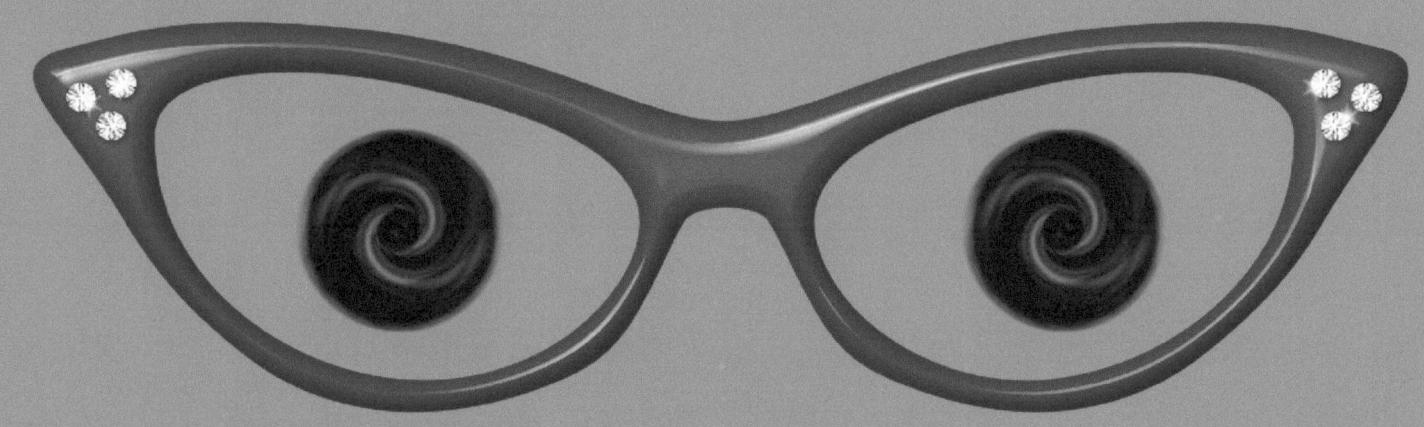

HOW TO FOCUS
AND BE INTENTIONAL

When it comes to driving your desires forward, **focus is vital**. Now, I know for many people, it doesn't come easy. You have so much on your plate already—careers, businesses, kids, friends, lives—you may find it challenging to do one more thing, no matter how badly you want it.

So how do you make it happen? The answer is pretty simple …

Make the room.

"Focus is only hard when your eyes are always wandering away from the task at hand."

Focus is only hard when your eyes are always wandering away from the task at hand. If you allow your mind, energy (and your hands) to veer off two lanes over, you'll never reach your destination.

You can do all of the affirming, planning, wishing and wanting you desire, but none of it matters if you don't create the space to plan your work and work your plan—undisturbed. Real talk, you are multi-tasking and multi-people-ing yourself into a perpetual state of no progress.

You see, focus comes when you choose the actions that move you closer to your ultimate goal and block out anything and everyone else until that thing gets done.

It's time to exercise your "no."

Refuse to allow other people, tasks, and even doubt to invade your space.

Now, hang this sign up on the door and don't look up until you've accomplished your goal:

DO NOT DISTURB. DESIRE MANIFESTATION IN PROGRESS.

WAYS THAT I CAN FOCUS
AND BE INTENTIONAL...

Desire

Why do you want this desire?

TODAY'S DATE:

WHAT IS BLOCKING YOUR ACCESS TO THIS DESIRE?

WHAT'S THE **PREPARATION** NEEDED TO GAIN ACCESS TO THIS **DESIRE?**

PLEASE WRITE DOWN YOUR ENTIRE ACTION PLAN
INCLUDE AS MANY DETAILS AS POSSIBLE

PLEASE WRITE DOWN YOUR ENTIRE ACTION PLAN
INCLUDE AS MANY DETAILS AS POSSIBLE

PLEASE WRITE DOWN YOUR ENTIRE ACTION PLAN
INCLUDE AS MANY DETAILS AS POSSIBLE

_____
_____
_____

PLEASE WRITE DOWN YOUR ENTIRE ACTION PLAN
INCLUDE AS MANY DETAILS AS POSSIBLE

DAILY *Affirmations* FOR THIS DESIRE

MONDAY:

TUESDAY:

WEDNESDAY:

THURSDAY:

FRIDAY:

SATURDAY:

SUNDAY:

DAILY Affirmations
FOR THIS DESIRE

MONDAY:

TUESDAY:

WEDNESDAY:

THURSDAY:

FRIDAY:

SATURDAY:

SUNDAY:

DAILY Affirmations
FOR THIS DESIRE

MONDAY:

TUESDAY:

WEDNESDAY:

THURSDAY:

FRIDAY:

SATURDAY:

SUNDAY:

DAILY *Affirmations* FOR THIS DESIRE

MONDAY:

TUESDAY:

WEDNESDAY:

THURSDAY:

FRIDAY:

SATURDAY:

SUNDAY:

Reflections Journal
FOR THIS DESIRE

WHEN DID YOU GET YOUR YES?

DATE:

TIME:

TELL THE STORY:

DATE:

TIME:

TELL THE STORY:

HOW DO YOU PLAN TO MAINTAIN THIS DESIRE?

HOW DO YOU PLAN TO MAINTAIN THIS DESIRE?

Desire

Why do you want this desire?

TODAY'S DATE:

WHAT IS BLOCKING YOUR ACCESS TO THIS DESIRE?

WHAT'S THE **PREPARATION** NEEDED TO GAIN ACCESS TO THIS **DESIRE?**

PLEASE WRITE DOWN YOUR ENTIRE ACTION PLAN
INCLUDE AS MANY DETAILS AS POSSIBLE

PLEASE WRITE DOWN YOUR ENTIRE ACTION PLAN
INCLUDE AS MANY DETAILS AS POSSIBLE

PLEASE WRITE DOWN YOUR ENTIRE ACTION PLAN
INCLUDE AS MANY DETAILS AS POSSIBLE

PLEASE WRITE DOWN YOUR ENTIRE ACTION PLAN
INCLUDE AS MANY DETAILS AS POSSIBLE

DAILY Affirmations FOR THIS DESIRE

MONDAY:

TUESDAY:

WEDNESDAY:

THURSDAY:

FRIDAY:

SATURDAY:

SUNDAY:

DAILY Affirmations FOR THIS DESIRE

MONDAY:

TUESDAY:

WEDNESDAY:

THURSDAY:

FRIDAY:

SATURDAY:

SUNDAY:

DAILY Affirmations FOR THIS DESIRE

MONDAY:

TUESDAY:

WEDNESDAY:

THURSDAY:

FRIDAY:

SATURDAY:

SUNDAY:

DAILY Affirmations FOR THIS DESIRE

MONDAY:

TUESDAY:

WEDNESDAY:

THURSDAY:

FRIDAY:

SATURDAY:

SUNDAY:

WHEN DID YOU GET YOUR YES?

DATE:

TIME:

TELL THE STORY:

TELL THE STORY:

HOW DO YOU PLAN TO MAINTAIN THIS DESIRE?

HOW DO YOU PLAN TO MAINTAIN THIS DESIRE?

Desire

Why DO YOU WANT THIS DESIRE?

TODAY'S DATE:

WHAT IS BLOCKING YOUR ACCESS TO THIS DESIRE?

WHAT'S THE **PREPARATION** NEEDED TO GAIN ACCESS TO THIS **DESIRE?**

PLEASE WRITE DOWN YOUR ENTIRE ACTION PLAN
INCLUDE AS MANY DETAILS AS POSSIBLE

_____

_____

_____

_____

_____

_____

_____

_____

_____

_____

PLEASE WRITE DOWN YOUR ENTIRE ACTION PLAN
INCLUDE AS MANY DETAILS AS POSSIBLE

PLEASE WRITE DOWN YOUR ENTIRE ACTION PLAN
INCLUDE AS MANY DETAILS AS POSSIBLE

_____

_____

_____

PLEASE WRITE DOWN YOUR ENTIRE ACTION PLAN

INCLUDE AS MANY DETAILS AS POSSIBLE

DAILY *Affirmations* FOR THIS DESIRE

MONDAY:

TUESDAY:

WEDNESDAY:

THURSDAY:

FRIDAY:

SATURDAY:

SUNDAY:

FOR THIS DESIRE

MONDAY:

TUESDAY:

WEDNESDAY:

THURSDAY:

FRIDAY:

SATURDAY:

SUNDAY:

DAILY *Affirmations* FOR THIS DESIRE

MONDAY:

TUESDAY:

WEDNESDAY:

THURSDAY:

FRIDAY:

SATURDAY:

SUNDAY:

DAILY *Affirmations* FOR THIS DESIRE

MONDAY:

TUESDAY:

WEDNESDAY:

THURSDAY:

FRIDAY:

SATURDAY:

SUNDAY:

DATE:

TIME:

TELL THE STORY:

HOW DO YOU PLAN TO MAINTAIN THIS DESIRE?

HOW DO YOU PLAN TO MAINTAIN THIS DESIRE?

Desire

Why DO YOU WANT THIS DESIRE?

TODAY'S DATE:

WHAT IS BLOCKING YOUR ACCESS TO THIS DESIRE?

WHAT'S THE **PREPARATION** NEEDED TO GAIN ACCESS TO THIS **DESIRE?**

PLEASE WRITE DOWN YOUR ENTIRE ACTION PLAN
INCLUDE AS MANY DETAILS AS POSSIBLE

_____

_____

_____

_____

_____

_____

_____

_____

_____

PLEASE WRITE DOWN YOUR ENTIRE ACTION PLAN
INCLUDE AS MANY DETAILS AS POSSIBLE

_____

_____

_____

_____

_____

_____

PLEASE WRITE DOWN YOUR ENTIRE ACTION PLAN
INCLUDE AS MANY DETAILS AS POSSIBLE

_____

_____

_____

PLEASE WRITE DOWN YOUR ENTIRE ACTION PLAN
INCLUDE AS MANY DETAILS AS POSSIBLE

DAILY *Affirmations* FOR THIS DESIRE

MONDAY:

TUESDAY:

WEDNESDAY:

THURSDAY:

FRIDAY:

SATURDAY:

SUNDAY:

DAILY *Affirmations*
FOR THIS DESIRE

MONDAY:

TUESDAY:

WEDNESDAY:

THURSDAY:

FRIDAY:

SATURDAY:

SUNDAY:

DAILY Affirmations
FOR THIS DESIRE

MONDAY:

TUESDAY:

WEDNESDAY:

THURSDAY:

FRIDAY:

SATURDAY:

SUNDAY:

DAILY *Affirmations* FOR THIS DESIRE

MONDAY:

TUESDAY:

WEDNESDAY:

THURSDAY:

FRIDAY:

SATURDAY:

SUNDAY:

Reflections
Journal
For This Desire

DATE:

TIME:

TELL THE STORY:

HOW DO YOU PLAN TO MAINTAIN THIS DESIRE?

HOW DO YOU PLAN TO MAINTAIN THIS DESIRE?

About the Author and Creator of The Yes Experience

She is a self-titled, results-validated Branding and Marketing Genius. She is a pace setter, a needle mover and an industry innovator. She is a woman with a master plan, a marketer with a message and the brains behind the brands of several industry influencers in the online realm.

She is **Audria Richmond.**

Audria is the founder of the Building Big Brands Agency, an award-winning branding and marketing consultancy for top-notch brands who want to command first-rate profits. As a highly sought after consultant, Audria champions entrepreneurs to stand in front of their brands— UnCloned and Unafraid to be seen. With her incomparable formula of innovation, unquenchable creativity and tech-savviness, Audria is a force that is impossible to reckon with. In 2016, she helped her clients to reel in over $1 million in profits and she's left her mark on personal and company brands all over the world, from the United States to Singapore.

Audria changed the game with her signature system, UnCloned: The Seven Phases of a Profitable Personal Brand, a revolutionary system that teaches clients how to build wildly profitable personal brands from the ground up with the proven practices, the tools and the strategies they need to go big and stay there.

Shortly after the release of her first bestselling book, Are You Ready for the Yes: How to Prep Your Brand for Lucrative Opportunities in January 2017, her second firestarter, UnCloned: Seven Epic (Un) Rules for Owning Your Shit hit hands and hearts in July 2017. Her most personal project to date, UnCloned has morphed into a massive, motivational movement, inspiring thousands of people to redefine the notion of normal and shake the shackles of conformity so they can embrace—and express—who they truly are.

She also lends her expertise and unconventional, never-inside-the-box perspective to Forbes Magazine's digital platform as a member of the Coaches Council.

Meet Audria at www.audriarichmond.com.

www.ingramcontent.com/pod-product-compliance
Lightning Source LLC
Chambersburg PA
CBHW041832300426
44111CB00002B/61